Bibliographic information published by the German National Library:

The German National Library lists this publication in the National Bibliography; detailed bibliographic data are available on the Internet at http://dnb.dnb.de .

Imprint:

Copyright © 2011 GRIN Verlag, Open Publishing GmbH
Print and binding: Books on Demand GmbH, Norderstedt Germany
ISBN: 9783668212688

This book at GRIN:

http://www.grin.com/en/e-book/321931/women-in-early-gothic-fiction-the-stereo-typical-depiction-of-women-as

Anonym

Women in Early Gothic Fiction. The stereotypical depiction of women as femmes fatales or damsels in distress in "The Italian" and "The Monk"

GRIN Publishing

GRIN - Your knowledge has value

Since its foundation in 1998, GRIN has specialized in publishing academic texts by students, college teachers and other academics as e-book and printed book. The website www.grin.com is an ideal platform for presenting term papers, final papers, scientific essays, dissertations and specialist books.

Visit us on the internet:

http://www.grin.com/

http://www.facebook.com/grincom

http://www.twitter.com/grin_com

Women in early Gothic Fiction

The depiction of women as femmes fatales and damsels in distress

Content

Women in early Gothic Fiction

1 Introduction

Catherine Morland is the young heroine of Jane Austen's novel *Northanger Abbey* that is probably the most famous parody on the Gothic Fiction stories which were pretty popular in the late 18th century. Catherine is likely the classic Gothic Fiction reader: naive, easy to excite and blessed with a strong imagination. Between the pages of her favourite novels she meets terrible villains, dark settings, mysterious secrets, adventurous flights, cold vaults, bad monks, bleeding nuns, heroic men and threatened maidens. She gets lost in those stories and the lines between her reality and the written fiction fade.

Of course Gothic novels are exciting and full of adventures, but a big part of their appeal comes from their characters. Especially the female ones are stereotypical and the different types are easy to find. So which females does Catherine meet while lying in the sun and enjoying a good novel? This seminar paper will show that there are really just two main stereotypes: the seductive "femme fatale" playing the role of the bad girl and the innocent "damsel in distress" as the good girl.

The two mentioned novels Catherine reads are *The Monk* by Matthew Lewis and *The Italian* by Ann Radcliffe which show these two opposite stereotypes of women pretty well. Both novels have examples for the damsel in distress but only *The Monk* gives one for the femme fatale. So this seminar paper will focus on Lewis' character Matilda as an example for the femme fatale and on Radcliffe's Ellena embodying the damsel in distress to explain the main theory: It is typical that women in early Gothic Fiction are either portrayed as femmes fatales or damsels in distress. In the following, this statement will be proved and studied. First of all, the content of both *The Italian* and *The Monk* will be shortly reviewed, the chosen women will be compared to each other in terms of both visual and characteristic descriptions. Then their relationships to other figures appearing in the stories will be analysed and in the end a brief conclusion will be drawn.

2 Summaries of primary literature

2.1 *The Italian* by Ann Radcliffe

The nobleman Vincentio di Vivaldi falls in love with Ellena di Rosalba who lives with her aunt Signora Bianchi and wants to marry her, but his mother is against their relationship and assigns a monk, Schedoni, to kidnap the poor Ellena. She escapes and Schedoni is instructed to assassinate her, but then he discovers that she is probably his daughter. The monk changes his plans immediately and safes her instead. After some troubles and hidden in a quite complex plot in which Ellena meets her real mother, it is revealed that she is only Schedoni's niece and that his dead brother was her real father. He belonged to an old, noble and wealthy family. Therefore, Ellena fits to Vivaldi's social standing and they marry. In the end everybody is happy.

2.2 *The Monk* by Matthew Lewis

The main plot tells the story of the devout Spanish monk Ambrosio who falls in love with a woman who comes to his monastery disguised as a young novice. The woman, Matilda, tempts him to break his celibacy. After he broke his vows by starting a sexual relationship with her, he wants to seduce the young and guiltless Antonia. Despite the fact that Matilda really loves Ambrosio, she helps him to accomplish his vicious goal with performing magical spells. With her aid, he is able to rape and kill Antonia. But then Ambrosio and Matilda are captured by the Inquisition and are tortured in order to confess all their sins. She tells her evils and gets burnt. Ambrosio escapes his death by selling his soul to the devil, but Satan reveals to him that his victim Antonia was his sister and that he sent Matilda especially to seduce him because he was too sinless in Satan's eyes. In the end, he dies a painful death to atone all his sins.

3 Ellena, the damsel in distress and Matilda, the femme fatale

Both Ellena and Matilda are important characters in the books they appear in but they interact in completely different ways. Women were - and still are - often discriminated by men, both in real life and as characters in novels. The reason for this is explained by Elvira Weißmann-Orzlowski in her book *Das Weibliche und die Unmöglichkeit seiner Integration*. She says, in reality as well as in literature, especially in early Gothic Fiction, men are afraid of women because of their ability to give birth to children and out of this fear they part them into stereotypes. These types are always opposite pairs: the saint and the sinner, the virgin and the whore or the angel and the witch. Women are extremes in their eyes; they are either extremely good or extremely bad persons. They are either innocent, pure and dependent on men or dangerous, seductive and independent. But they cannot be both good and bad at the same time (vgl. Weißmann-Orzlowski 1997, S. 23 ff.). Both the femme fatale and the damsel in distress cannot only be found in early Gothic Fiction but also in many other kinds of novels and stories through the many decades of writing.

Radcliffe's Ellena is the perfect example for the damsel in distress, threatened maiden, sentimental heroine or classic young virtuous heroine while Lewis' Matilda embodies the femme fatale, the vamp or the demon lover.

The damsel in distress is fast described: a young, innocent, virtuous girl who needs to be saved out of a dangerous situation - by a potential husband, if possible. She is beautiful but she would never use her beauty or her sexuality to reach her goals which are becoming a good mother and an even better housewife.

A short description of the femme fatale and her intentions is given here: "The protagonist's fall is sometimes accomplished through a relationship with a "demon lover" who acts as the protagonist's double or alter-ego, leading the protagonist into experiences forbidden by societal norms. The demon lover is frequently female, a femme fatale (fatal or deadly woman) who seduces and entices the protagonist to destruction" (http://resources.mhs.vic.edu.au/ creating/ pages/origins.htm).

3.1 Outer Appearance

Considering the fact that women were - and still are - judged by their beauty, no reader would like to hear a story about an ugly heroine no matter how evil or pure she is. Both Ellena and Matilda are especially beautiful and have wonderful voices which match their attention-drawing appearances. In each novel the reader gets to know their looks through the eyes of a male character: Vivaldi in Ellena's and Ambrosio in Matilda's case. But before they really see the women, they both hear their voices which seem to be an important factor of beauty.

When Ambrosio hears Matilda sing, "he wondered how such heavenly sounds could be produced by any but angels" (Lewis 2009, S. 60). While Vivaldi is fascinated by "the sweetness and fine expression of her [Ellena's] voice" (Radcliffe 2011, S. 9).

Even if Ellena and Matilda embody opposite stereotypes, their voices are similar to each other. But Matilda is aware of how her voice attracts other people and uses it to seduce Ambrosio. She sings a song for him and accompanies herself with a harp which "prove[s] her a perfect mistress of the instrument" (Lewis 2009, S. 57). Ambrosio is captured by her whole performance and starts feeling sexually drawn to her. While singing, the reader catches the very first glimpse at her face: "Two coral lips were visible, ripe, fresh, and melting, and a chin in whose dimples seemed to lurk a thousand cupids" (Lewis 2009, S. 60). And it goes on with the description of her arms, the only parts of her body not covered by the dark monk habit she is wearing because "she had drawn it [the sleeve] above her elbow" (Lewis 2009, S. 60). So the reader follows Ambrosio's eyes and sees "an arm [...] formed in the most perfect symmetry, the delicacy of whose skin might have contended with snow in whiteness" (Lewis 2009, S. 60). Ambrosio slowly starts falling for her in this moment. Later, we discover her face, which is similar to the face of the picture of the Madonna that Ambrosio is always starring at and having sexual fantasies about. This Madonna "which for two years has been an object of his adoration" (Andriano 1993, S. 34) embodies his perfect idol of a woman and his hidden sexual desires. As Joseph Andriano writes in his book *Our ladies of darkness*: "In the beginning of the novel, he [Ambrosio] is so proud of his celibacy that he considers himself immune to sexual temptation; he feels superior to other men" (Andriano 1993, S. 34). But this feeling of immunity fades more and more; first when he is alone in his room with the painted Madonna and then in the physical presence of Matilda. Later, the reader finally is allowed to see her complete face through Ambrosio's eyes: "The same exquisite proportion of features, the same profusion of golden hair, the same rosy lips, heavenly eyes" (Lewis 2009, S. 62) as his beloved Madonna. There is no doubt that Matilda is especially beautiful and Ambrosio is overwhelmed by her beauty. All his attempts to do the right thing and throw her out of the monastery fail and in the end it is no problem for her anymore to seduce him and make him break his vows.

Contrary to Matilda's, Ellena's outer beauty is described very early in *The Italian*. The reader gets his or her first impression of Ellena just based on her looks after the brief introduction through her voice without any description of her personal traits. Her physical appearance seems to be her most important good and Vivaldi falls in love with her because of her "figure, which had a distinguished air of delicacy and grace" (Radcliffe 2011, S. 10). He is not falling for Ellena because of her personality but because of her looks who are later pictured to be "more touchingly beautiful that he had dared to image" (Radcliffe 2011, S. 9).

The message the reader gets is that a woman is something to look at but nothing that is responsible for bigger influences on life in general. Vivaldi sees her as a piece of decoration that he wants to look at. Ellena is judged by her beauty and her following role in the novel is sealed. Her angel-like beauty shows her innocence even more than just her character. She would never use her looks to influence someone, neither in a positive nor in a negative way.

When Ellena becomes aware of how her beauty is affecting Vivaldi "she hastily drew her veil" (Radcliffe 2011, S. 10) to conceal her face again and especially "her dark blue eyes [which] sparkled with intelligence" (Radcliffe 2011, S. 10) to stop confusing him with her looks. Even if Ellena's voice first draws Vivaldi's attention towards herself, it is her beauty that makes him fall for her completely. But actually "she is a cipher: the passive beautiful orphan waiting to be rescued by the handsome hero" (White 2011, S. ix). Still, "her features were of the Grecian outline, and [...] they expressed the tranquillity of an elegant mind" (Radcliffe 2011, S. 10), which describes her to be intelligent, but this doesn't save her from being in need later in the novel.

A damsel in distress is not necessarily a stupid or simple-minded girl, even the most clever ones can be pressed into the stereotypical forms in which authors tend to part their characters. As shown above, the biggest difference between Matilda's and Ellena's outer appearance is the way in which they use their beauty. Matilda uses hers as a weapon on her way to her goal and Ellena tries to cover hers up, but the reader still judges her by it because of the different ways the characters are described and introduced into their stories.

Beauty is of course an important factor for both women in real life and for the fictional ones, and it can be used as something good and as something bad. After all every character consists of more parts than just his or her outer appearance and the description of their physical appearances is yet very important for the reader to imagine the character right. Which is the reason for looking closer at the personal traits and the way Ellena and Matilda react and act during the novels.

3.2 Characterization

To truly understand what the story does to a character and its personal development, two fixed terms should be defined: The term "flat character" and the term "round character".

The first one is "a minor character in a work of fiction who does not undergo substantial change or growth in the course of a story" (http://fictionwriting.about.com/od/glossary/g/ flatcharacters.htm). The second one is "a major character in a work of fiction who encounters conflict and is changed by it" (http://fictionwriting.about.com/od/glossary/g/RoundCharacter. htm).

The interaction of Matilda and Ellena during their stories is very opposite: First Matilda is a flat character as she is disguised as a boy and the reader does not give this young novice his or her attention. As the story goes on, she becomes more and more a round character and her real goals are only revealed in the very end of *The Monk*.

Ellena's journey through *The Italian* starts with her being a round character which seems to be surprising as she embodies the classic damsel in distress. But as Kathryn White writes in her introduction to *The Italian* about her: "She does have inner strengths and independent characteristics" (White 2011, ix). To reach the goal that is given to her as a stereotypical character; finding a rich and good-looking man and becoming his wife, she goes the way from a round character down to a flat character (vgl. Weißmann-Orzlowski 1997, S. 140).

Both women go through a kind of development, but their directions are opposite. If the reader takes a closer look at Ellena, he or she will see that she does not match into the stereotype entirely in the beginning of the novel as she earns her own living which was not acceptable for a young and respectable woman in the late 18th century. For Ellena herself, working and making a living from it, is nothing to be ashamed of but still she suffers from the contempt other people have for her (vgl. Weißmann-Orzlowski 1997, S. 142). During the novel she slowly loses her self-esteem and independence to become the ideal housewife. Finally, Ellena becomes a typical Gothic damsel in distress who embodies the ideal woman both in Ann Radcliffe's time and in the time her novel is set in. From today's feministic point of view she failed and was not able to emancipate herself completely. But as soon as the reader changes his or her point of view back to the one from the late 18th century, she succeeded in the way her character changed. An independent woman who earns her own money and does not need a man was not accepted by society in the real world nor in the fictional world that is created in *The Italian*. The author Ann Radcliffe changes Ellena from the strong young woman to the modest wife of Vivaldi to let the other characters and society be able to accept her. This changes feels like a hard break for modern readers but it was necessary for Ellena's future in the novel as she has to live her whole life in a male-dominated world (vgl. Weißmann-Orzlowski 1997, S. 150-151). This change starts as soon as Ellena begins to use typical female ways of influencing people. She cries and faints for example. As Elvira Weißmann-Orzlowski writes: "Mit dem Einsetzen der weiblichen Waffen des Weinens und der Ohnmacht beginnt folgerichtig Ellenas Regression zum flat character, was sich auch im Ansteigen ihrer Ängste zeigt" (Weißmann-Orzlowski 1997, S. 145). She stops to think on her own and suddenly is in need to be saved. As Elvira Weißmann-Orzlowski writes sarcastically: "In *The Italian* spielen gute weibliche Charaktere keine bedeutende Rolle. Darüber hinaus sind sie unrealistisch angelegt" (Weißmann-Orzlowski 1997, S. 124). Ellena never had a chance to emancipate herself and stay independent as the author always had her in mind as a damsel in distress.

Whereas Matilda makes her journey the other way round: she is a flat character in first place and then she becomes a round character as the story goes on and starts revealing her personality more and more. Matilda doesn't care for society's acceptance as her goal is not to become a perfect housewife. In this part of her personality, her attitude is very modern. She controls the male characters and she is not controlled by them. But the author does not make her an appealing role-model for women. Matilda embodies the evil and the independence she takes from her sexuality and the way she uses her beauty to get what she wants are shown in a negative way. Even the femme fatale is not allowed to do what she wants. She has to suffer like every other woman and probably even more because of her sins as she is portrayed as "die kraftvolle, sexuell aktive Frau […] die weiß, was sie will und die danach handelt" (Weißmann-Orzlowski 1997, S. 116). The femme fatale is the opposite of the damsel in distress if it comes to her traits and development. Matilda goes through three changes during the novel and after every single one, she is portrayed even more evil: first she is disguised as a boy, then it is revealed that she is a woman and in the end she is just a non-human demon (vgl. Weißmann-Orzlowski 1997, S. 100). But as a femme fatale she is not treated different from the damsel in distress: No matter what kind of stereotypical woman a female character in early Gothic Fiction is and if she is a good or evil person, she has to subordinate herself under the rules the male characters make. Even in her complete evilness, Matilda still has to suffer emotionally: She really falls in love with Ambrosio and he does not return this love, but instead he uses her to get what he wants. As Elvira Weißmann-Orzlowski writes: "Matilda verkörpert den Typus der femme fatale, von dem sich männlicher Überlegenheitswahn bedroht fühlt" (Weißmann-Orzlowski 1997, S. 108). The author literally punishes her for being the femme fatale he made her for his story.

3.3 Relationships to other characters

To truly understand how a character acts, one must look at the relationships he or she has to the other characters in the novel. Matilda and Ellena are surrounded by different men and women who influence them in their reactions. Some are relatives, some are villains, some are friends and many of them and their relationships to other characters change during the novel. In the following, the connections between the example femme fatale and the example damsel in distress will be analysed. First the ones they have with the other female characters and then the ones with the male characters.

3.3.1 To female characters

Matilda and Ellena meet a lot of other female characters while developing and changing. A big part of these characters are mothers or mother figures. In her book *The matrophobic Gothic and its legacy* Deborah Rogers explains the importance of the mother-daughter-relationship in Gothic Fiction very well. She explains that many characteristic traits of damsels in distress come from their bad relationships to their mothers. The word she uses for this is "matrophobic" which she explains in the beginning of her book as "the fear of mothers, the fear of becoming a mother, the fear of identification with and separation from the maternal body" (vgl. Rogers 2007, S. 1).

It it also an interesting aspect that damsels in distress seem to suffer under their bad mother-daughter-bonds, while the reader never gets any information on how a femme fatale got along with her mother. But the fact that the early lives and the familiar roots of femmes fatales are always very mysterious and hidden in the dark make them probably even more appealing for men.

It is important to know that "female identity is established through bonds with other women, especially maternal figures" (Rogers 2007, S.39). If the reader takes a closer look on Ellena's mother and maternal figures in *The Italian* he or she will undoubtedly notice that Ellena was not lucky with her relationships. In the beginning of the novel, Ellena lives with her aunt Signora Bianchi who is like a mother to her. Ellena's real mother also appears in the end of the novel but the reader does not immediately learn who she is and why she did not take care for Ellena on her own. Signora Bianchi raised Ellena since she was a child and told her that she is an orphan. They live together and have a good relationship. As earlier explained, Ellena works to earn money as the women are not very rich. Unfortunately the author lets the poor aunt die in a very mysterious way instead of giving the reader a chance to get to know her better. But before she dies, Signora Bianchi promises Vivaldi Ellena's hand and therefore she acts as her mother. She even acts like a father as it was usually his task in a time of patriarchy to find a husband for his daughter and promise the lucky chosen man her hand. After Signora Bianchi gives Vivaldi the promise that allows him to marry Ellena, he quickly thinks that the aunt must have had some thoughts about her own probably close death which would "leave Ellena a young and friendless orphan" (Radcliffe 2011, S.31). The reader sees through Vivaldi's mind that Signora Bianchi really acts through motherly love for Ellena as she thinks about the time of Ellena's life when she is gone and not there to share a house and a living with her. Even though Signora Bianchi did not give birth to Ellena and is therefore not her biological mother, she cares a lot more for her as her real mother Olivia who lives as a nun.

They are even friends and yet Olivia does not recognise Ellena to be her daughter. It takes the servant Beatrice to open her eyes. What kind of mother is she when she does not identify her own daughter when she sees her? But according to Deborah Rogers this should not surprise the reader as "Radcliffe's novels [...] systematically displace, silence, or devalue the figure of the mother" (Rogers 2007, S.9). After Ellena finds out that Olivia is her mother, there are no signs that the relationship between them changes.

A part of the personality of those not well-mothered women that are turned into damsels in distress by the author is not finished. And this little lack in their personality makes them weak and the reader pities them for growing up without a good mother who takes care of them. The damsel in distress develops a "female sensibility that encourages passivity and depression" (Rogers 2007, S.38). This sensibility makes her so passive that she needs to be saved by the male hero of the story.

The femme fatale Matilda on the other hand does not have close relationships with any other female character. She comes to the monastery disguised as a male novice and the reader never sees her interacting with another woman or girl. A huge part of the personality of a femme fatale is her interaction with male characters as she is the kind of woman men are afraid of, but still secretly dream about.

3.3.2 To male characters

As explained earlier, the female characters have to subordinate themselves under the male ones and their ideas of how a woman is supposed to be.

A femme fatale like Matilda is not willing to subordinate herself under the rules of others; no matter if they are male or female. But still without men she cannot exist as this stereotype is based on the effect that women have on the male characters. In Matilda's case it is Ambrosio who is her counterpart. She needs him to go further in her personal development to a round character as the novel goes on. The man who is seduced by the femme fatale says a lot about her personality. The problem is that even when Ambrosio and Matilda share a relationship like lovers, they do not have the same feelings for each other. While Matilda is replaceable for Ambrosio and his feelings are not bound to her as a person, Matilda really loves him. As she is sent by the devil to tempt the too sinless Ambrosio it may seem surprising that she is able to feel like a human being and really fall in love with the monk. But after all the reader should keep in mind that the author tries to portray every woman who does not fit into the social standards of his time even more evil. But actually Ambrosio is the evil one as he always blames the women for his wrongdoings. He sleeps with Matilda and he rapes Antonia, but afterwards the women are accused of being the bad ones. Elvira Weißmann-Orzlowski explains this circumstances like this: "Die Schuld, die die Frauen auf sich geladen haben, besteht in ihrem Frau-sein, ihrer Schönheit und in ihrer mehr oder minder zufälligen Anwesenheit in seiner [Ambrosios] Gegenwart" (Weißmann-Orzlowski 1997, S. 116). The male-dominated society has found a simple way of blaming women in making their fault their beauty. Suddenly, Ambrosio is the victim even if he was the one who raped and killed Antonia and Matilda is the culprit.

If the reader takes a closer look at Ellena and what position a damsel in distress takes in a relationship with a male character, he or she will notice that men will do everything to prevent the damsel from emancipating herself. In the beginning of *The Italian* both Vivaldi and Schedoni need Ellena, but she does not require any of them. She is free and therefore the story has to make her dependent on men to make her fit into the given social standards. First Schedoni takes her personal freedom in kidnapping her and in the end Vivaldi marries her which takes Ellena's freedom away again (vgl. Weißmann-Orzlowski 1997, S. 150-151). Some even say she gets simply boring after marrying her Prince Charming. Elvira Weißmann-Orzlowski states ironically: "Der differenzierte Charakter der Heldin erhält nach der Hochzeit eine gewisse Flachheit. Sie wird zur idealen Ehefrau, unbehelligt von den Leidenschaften, die sie vorher hin- und herwarfen. Kurz: Sie wird langweilig" (Weißmann-Orzlowski 1997, S. 151). It is interesting how the relationship between the monk Schedoni who seems to be the villain at first and Ellena changes during the course of the novel. Ellena is portrayed as an orphan in the beginning and in the end she meets her mother and also finds out who her father was. Schedoni is actually her uncle and not her father which is what he first assumes. While he questions her about her father she answers to him "I never knew a father's care […] nor till lately did I perceive the want of it" (Radcliffe 2011, S. 265). This quote shows the change in her character a lot: After all these years without a father by her side, she suddenly feels the need of one. The father represents the patriarchy of society and when Ellena is missing him, she also misses the social standards. It looks like that she really wants to subordinate herself under the male characters. Schedoni on the other hand is completely surprised when he finds out that Ellena could probably be his daughter. He even shows really deep emotions and changes from the villain to a feeling human being as Ellena "perceived tears swell in his eyes, which were fixed on hers" (Radcliffe 2011, S. 266). But even if his feelings towards her shift, he still embodies the society that keeps Ellena from releasing herself into freedom.

The relationships between the different characters in both novels are complicated and confusing. No matter how often the reader will try to understand them entirely, he or she will likely fail.

4. Conclusion

The image of women in early Gothic Fiction is a complex and not very positive one. While reading Gothic novels the modern reader will undoubtedly search for nice and appealing females who are portrayed as strong and independent women. In early Gothic Fiction this search will not be successful. Those books were written in another time when society and the role allocation between men and women were different. Still there were a few ironic authors who dared to make fun of Gothic Fiction in a time when it was very up to date to read such novels.

Jane Austen for example parodies this image in the already mentioned *Northanger Abbey* with creating a female main character that is even more innocent and dewy-eyed than the average damsel in distress. Catherine Morland is the perfect Gothic Fiction reader and should open everybody's eyes on the flaws of this genre.

Other authors like Mary Shelley and Bram Stoker took the stereotypes to the next level.

I n *Frankenstein* Shelley makes her damsel in distress Elizabeth even more passive and defenceless and kills her in the end as one of the probably flattest female character that ever appears in Gothic Fiction.

Stoker carries his femmes fatales in the shape of female vampires in *Dracula* to the extremes (vgl. Weißmann-Orzlowski 1997, S. 246-249).

There are also a few female characters that cannot be put into the explained stereotypes such as Cathy in Emily Bronte's *Wuthering Heights* or Rosemary in Ira Levin's *Rosemary's Baby*.

Later, the reader will meet more positive female characters in Gothic literature such as Charlotte Brontë's Jane Eyre who acts according to her principles in the same-named novel.

In the *Harry Potter* Series which is the newest and probably most famous row of Gothic Fiction novels, the reader meets Hermione Granger who is definitely not a damsel in distress and knows very well how to take care of herself.

Every reader and lover of Gothic Fiction should keep in mind what Henry Tilney, the main male character in *Northanger Abbey* tells Catherine Morland about her too strong admiration of the Gothic: "What have you been judging from? Remember the country and the age we live in" (Austen 2003, S. 186).

Those are just novels; the times have changed and so have the images of women in literature.

Bibliography of Books

Andriano, Joseph: Our ladies of darkness, Pennsylvania State University Press, Pennsylvania 1993.

Austen, Jane: Northanger Abbey, Penguin Classics, Reissue 2003.

Lewis, Matthew Gregory: The Monk, Wordsworth Editions Limited, 2009.

Radcliffe, Ann: The Italian, Wordsworth Editions Limited, 2011.

Rogers, Deborah D.: The matrophobic gothic and its legacy, New York, NY [u.a.], Lang, 2007.

Weißmann-Orzlowski, Elvira: Das Weibliche und die Unmöglichkeit seiner Integration, Frankfurt am Main [u.a.], Lang, 1997.

White, Kathryn: Introduction, in: Radcliffe, Anne: The Italian, Wordsworth Editions Limited, 2011.

Bibliography of Online Sources

Marotous, George (u.a.): Textual Characteristics of the Gothic, http://resources.mhs.vic.edu.au/creating/pages/origins.htm (Stand: 30.10.2011)

The New York Times Company (Hrsg.): Definition: Flat Chracter, http://fictionwriting.about.com/od/glossary/g/flatcharacters.htm (Stand: 04.11.2011)

The New York Times Company (Hrsg.): Definition: Round Character, http://fictionwriting.about.com/od/glossary/g/RoundCharacter.htm (Stand: 04.11.2011)

YOUR KNOWLEDGE HAS VALUE